SANKOFA
BLACK HERITAGE COLLECTION

EARLY CIVILIZATIONS OF AFRICA

ADRIENNE SHADD

SERIES EDITOR • TOM HENDERSON

Funded by the
Government
of Canada | Canada

www.rubiconpublishing.com I www.savvas.com

Associate Publisher: Amy Land
Project Editor: Jessica Rose
Editorial Assistant: Sarah Adams
Creative Director: Jennifer Drew
Lead Designer: Sherwin Flores
Graphic Designers: Jen Harvey, Megan Little, Jason Mitchell

Every reasonable effort has been made to trace the owners of copyrighted
material and to make due acknowledgement. Any errors or omissions
drawn to our attention will be gladly rectified in future editions.

22 23 24 25 26   10 9 8 7 6

ISBN: 978-1-77058-829-5

Printed in Canada

CONTENTS

EARLY CIVILIZATIONS OF AFRICA

A region's identity is shaped partly by its history. Learning about the past helps us to understand the modern world. Lessons from long ago can also guide us in solving problems today. In this book, you'll learn about early African civilizations. These incredible civilizations have influenced life around the world.

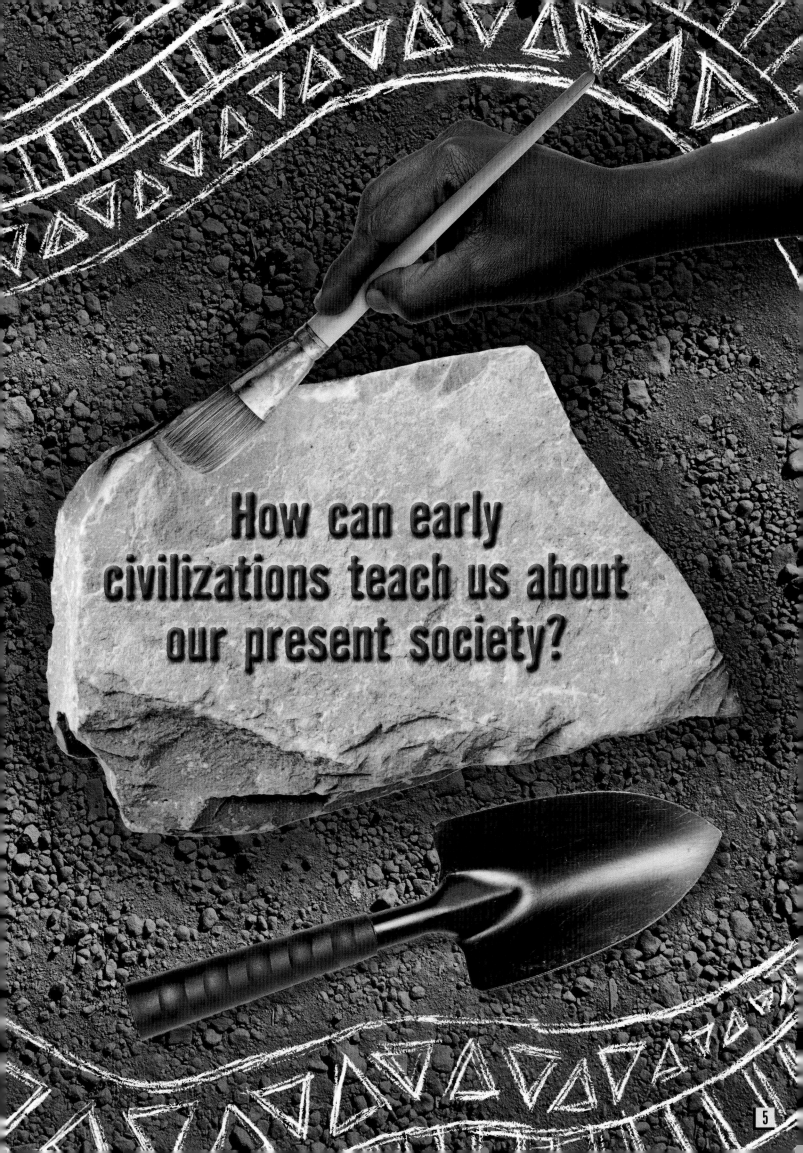

How can early civilizations teach us about our present society?

Great Moments in Africa's Ancient History

THINK ABOUT IT

What do you know about ancient Africa? Share your thoughts in a small group.

AFRICA HAS A long and impressive history. Read this timeline to learn about the key events that helped shape the continent. Since many of the events in this timeline happened so far back in time, it is difficult to know exactly when each event took place. The dates in the following entries are approximate times when each kingdom, culture, event, or ruler existed.

The oldest fossils of *Homo sapiens*, or modern humans, date back almost 200 000 years to Ethiopia. *Homo sapiens* originate in Africa, and spread to many parts of the world.

195 000 BCE

The first Egyptian pyramids are built. Imhotep, an architect, doctor, and priest, improves pyramid construction by using stone instead of mud. Huge advances in navigation, astronomy, and medicine are made during this time.

astronomy: *science that deals with space, planets, stars, and the universe*

2775 – 2250 BCE

9000 – 3000 BCE

Human beings move from hunting and gathering to domesticating animals and growing crops.

3000 BCE

The civilization of ancient Egypt begins in northeast Africa. We see the first appearance of Egyptian writing, known as hieroglyphics.

25th dynasty pharaoh as a sphinx

767 – 671 BCE

The kingdom of Kush, located in modern-day Sudan, reunifies and rules Egypt during the 25th dynasty. This is known as the period of the "Black Pharaohs" because of the conquerors' dark skin.

reunifies: *brings together again*

The kingdom of Kush is defeated by the Assyrian Empire, centred in what is now Iraq. The kingdom of Kush moves to Meroe, a city farther south along the Nile. The Meroites rival Egypt in terms of wealth and culture.

700 BCE – 300 CE

100 – 500s to 900s CE

The kingdom of Aksum flourishes in the area of modern-day Ethiopia. It is known for erecting many stelae, or granite columns, which still stand today. One of these columns is 27 metres tall and is the largest of its kind in the world.

King Ezana's stela, located in the Northern Stelae Park, is one of the columns in Aksum.

The ancient Nok culture thrives in the forests of central Nigeria. The Nok people are admired for their art and sculptures.

500 BCE to 200s CE

400 – 1200s CE

Ancient Ghana, 650 kilometres north of modern-day Ghana, becomes a major trading empire, getting its power and wealth from gold.

500 – 400 BCE

Iron melting is practised in what is now Nigeria, central Niger, and southern Mali. Armed with this technology, people spread across Africa.

Moors, or early Muslim Africans, invade Spain. They bring agriculture, mining, industry, manufacturing, architecture, and higher learning to Spain. Spain is the centre of culture and learning throughout Europe for almost 800 years.

Muslim: *follower of the religion of Islam*

740 CE

Ife bronze casting of a king dated around the 12th century

The Yoruba kingdoms of Ife and Benin in what is now Nigeria are believed to have been founded. The city of Timbuktu, which later becomes a great centre of trade and learning, is established in Mali.

Sundiata Keita comes to power in 1235 and rules over the empire of Mali. Over the next few hundred years, the city of Timbuktu is transformed into a major centre of trade and learning. It is home to the world's first university. Gold and the salt trade are very important for the empire.

1100

1235 – 1600

800 CE – 1800s

Kanem-Bornu, an African trading empire, is ruled by the Sef dynasty from the mid-9th to 19th centuries in the area around Lake Chad.

An illustration of Kanembu warriors and their mounted chief

1200s to 1500s

Great Zimbabwe flourishes in southern Africa. Its people build the largest medieval stone structure south of the Sahara. It is the centre of a vast international trade system and covers a huge area between the Zambezi and Limpopo Rivers.

The Great Enclosure, part of the Great Zimbabwe ruins

Mansa Musa, a successor of Sundiata, rules Mali. In 1324, he makes a famous pilgrimage to Mecca. Mansa Musa brings back so much gold that its price falls in the Mediterranean.

As Mali declines, the Songhai (also spelled Songhay) empire rises to power. King Sonni Ali Ber comes to power around 1464. He and his successor extend their rule over an area larger than Mali or Ghana before it. Songhai is its strongest in the 15th and 16th centuries.

1464 – 1600

1324

1581 – 1663

Queen Nzinga of the Mbundu people of what is now Angola is an exceptional stateswoman and military strategist. During her rule, the Portuguese are not able to conquer the country.

Statue of Queen Nzinga in Luanda, Angola

1460

The Portuguese arrive on the coast of West Africa. They encounter large cities that are technologically advanced and well organized.

CONNECT IT

This timeline captures Africa's long history. Research one of the entries included on this timeline. Write a short report about the additional details you find about the person, kingdom, or event you research.

The KINGDOMS of EARLY AFRICA

MANY OF AFRICA'S early communities were the first in the world. In fact, the oldest human fossils have been found in Africa. The early kingdoms of Africa influenced many other civilizations that came after them. Look at the map below to learn more.

Since these civilizations date very far back in time, it is difficult to know the exact dates when they existed. Researchers have suggested many different dates for the following civilizations. Many of the dates below are times when each kingdom or empire was at its strongest.

THINK ABOUT IT

In a continent as large as Africa, what differences do you think there would be among kingdoms? What similarities might there be?

Ghana (400–700 CE to 1200 CE)

Although the kingdom of Ghana shares its name with present-day Ghana, the two are not the same. The kingdom of Ghana was about 650 km northwest of present-day Ghana. Gold was a major part of Ghana's economy, and it was used to trade with other kingdoms. Historical records say that Ghana had the richest gold mines in the world.

Songhai (1450 CE to 1600 CE)

This kingdom began as a state near a city called Gao in the early 1000s CE. Songhai was ruled by Mali until the mid-1400s. This kingdom rose to power through its growth and expanded trade with other lands. Songhai was home to the city of Timbuktu, the centre of knowledge for the region. Timbuktu is still a major city today in the country of Mali.

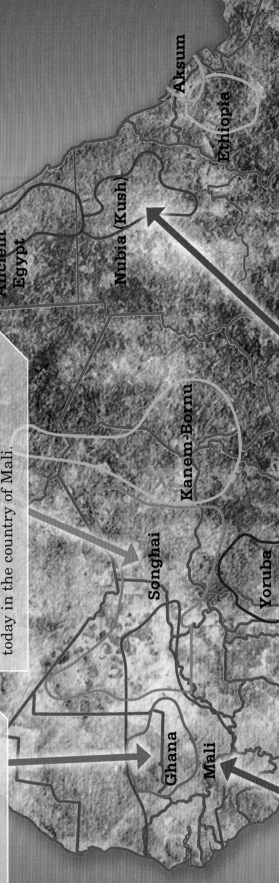

Ancient Egypt

Nubia (Kush)

Aksum

Ethiopia

Kanem-Bornu

Songhai

Yoruba

Ghana

Mali

Rwanda

Luba

Lunda

Kongo

Malawi

Kilwa

Merina

Zulu

Zimbabwe

Mali (1200 CE to 1550 CE)

Mali was first settled around 200 BCE, long before it became an official kingdom. Mali took over Ghana in the early 1200s. Mali was a wealthy kingdom because of its gold and salt trade. Mansa Musa, the richest person in all of history, was king of Mali from 1312 CE to 1337 CE. Parts of this kingdom still exist in present-day Mali.

Nubia, also known as Kush (6000 BCE to 1500 CE)

Nubia was located along the Nile River and had very close ties with Egypt. Nubia was a wealthy kingdom, mostly because of its gold. This kingdom was the first in the world to be ruled by a monarch. Kush, a kingdom within Nubia, lasted from 850 BCE to 350 CE. Kush came to replace the name Nubia when referring to the civilization.

monarch: *king, queen, emperor, or empress who rules over a kingdom or empire*

Zimbabwe (1220 CE to 1450 CE)

Like other African kingdoms, Zimbabwe traded gold and ivory with other kingdoms. Zimbabwe was made up of 150 tributaries, or states, that paid taxes to the king. The kingdom was best known for its many large stone structures. Many of these ancient stone ruins can still be seen today.

Because of the close relationship between Nubia and Egypt, Nubian people were often shown in Egyptian hieroglyphics. These hieroglyphics show Nubian people in the mid-1300s BCE.

CONNECT IT

Go online and research one of the other kingdoms shown on this map. Write a short fact card about your findings, and then share your fact card with a partner.

WOMEN IN ANCIENT EGYPT

THINK ABOUT IT

Imagine you were a woman living in ancient Egpyt. What do you think your life would be like?

EGYPT MAY BE well known for its large pyramids and ancient mummies. However, there's a lot more to this civilization. Egypt's ancient technological advances helped shape our modern world.

Ancient Egypt was ahead of its time. Women in Egypt held a unique position when compared to women in other societies of the ancient world. In some ways, they were very traditional, but, in other ways, they were remarkably modern. Read this report to learn more about the lives of women in ancient Egypt.

THE LAW

Women in ancient Egypt were equal to men before the law. They could own and rent property under their own name, borrow money, sign contracts, appear in court as witnesses, and start divorce proceedings. Women in the Western world did not achieve these rights for thousands of years.

A model of women workers grinding, baking, and brewing, 1900–1800 BCE

WORK

Most of the work done by women was in the home. This work included cooking, cleaning, washing clothes, and taking care of children. Women also worked in the fields and went to market. They could also work outside the home in certain occupations. A woman could work as a priestess, midwife, mourner, dancer, or musician. Even though women could hold some jobs, most occupations in public life were not open to them.

MARRIAGE

Egyptian women had the right to decide if they wanted to get married. They could decide who their partner would be. Unlike other ancient civilizations, women in ancient Egypt were not forced into marriage. However, they usually married very young, around the ages of 12 to 14. Love and affection were important in Egyptian marriages.

CHILDREN

In ancient Egypt, pregnancy tests told women if they were expecting a baby. When a pregnant woman urinated on wheat or barley, her hormones would cause the plants to sprout. It was also thought that the sex of the unborn baby could be determined. If the barley grew first, it would be a boy. If the wheat grew first, it would be a girl. Children were very important in the Egyptian world.

Wheat seeds   *Barley seeds*

WOMEN IN POWER

There were four female rulers in ancient Egypt. They were Nitocris, who ruled around 2180 BCE, Sebeknefru, who ruled around 1790 BCE, Hatshepsut, who ruled around 1479 BCE, and Tausert, who ruled around 1187 BCE. However, a queen who was the main wife of a king also enjoyed a great deal of power. For example, Queen Nefertiti (1370 BCE to 1330 BCE) advised her husband in matters of state.

A stone statue of Hatshepsut

FASHION AND MAKEUP

Egyptian women wore many different kinds of jewellery, including bead necklaces, earrings, bracelets, armlets, and anklets. On their heads, women wore headdresses and wigs. Men also wore jewellery and wigs. Both women and men also applied makeup made of ground minerals mixed with fat or oil.

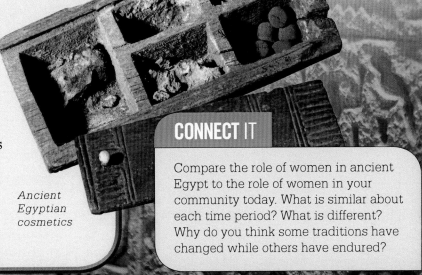

Ancient Egyptian cosmetics

CONNECT IT

Compare the role of women in ancient Egypt to the role of women in your community today. What is similar about each time period? What is different? Why do you think some traditions have changed while others have endured?

13

Cool Facts About
ANCIENT NUBIA

**ANCIENT
EGYPT**

NILE RIVER

Nubian archer sculptures

Nubian pyramids in Meroe

**ANCIENT
NUBIA**

MEROE

This iron grooming kit dates back to 200–300 CE.

THINK ABOUT IT

Why do you think some civilizations are better known than others? What might be the consequences of studying only well-known societies?

ANCIENT EGYPT WASN'T the only early society to make an impact on the world. According to Boston's Museum of Fine Arts, an earlier civilization called Nubia (also known as Kush) began in 6000 BCE. This dates the creation of Nubia thousands of years before the first communities in Egypt. Read this list to find out more.

1. "LAND OF THE BOW"

Ancient Egyptians referred to Nubia as "Ta-Seti" (or "Ta-Sety"), meaning "land of the bow." This is because many expert archers lived there. Some Nubian archers were even used in Egyptian armies.

2. NUBIA HAD MORE PYRAMIDS THAN EGYPT.

Egypt is known for its great pyramids, but Nubia had pyramids as well. Many of Nubia's pyramids are found in the ancient city of Meroe. Like the pyramids in Egypt, the pyramids in Meroe were used as royal tombs and monuments. Approximately 223 pyramids have been found in Nubia. This is roughly double the number found in Egypt.

3. NUBIANS WERE TALENTED CRAFTSPEOPLE.

The people of Nubia were very skilled metalworkers and artists. This is shown in the many artifacts found in Nubia today. One artifact, an ancient grooming set, included a tool similar to modern tweezers. Nubians were also known for their pottery.

CONNECT IT

The history of ancient Nubia spans thousands of years. Go online and find another interesting fact about Nubia. Write a short entry about it to add to this list.

WARRIOR QUEEN NZINGA

THINK ABOUT IT

Think of a woman you look up to in your life. Share your thoughts in a small group.

ONE OF THE MOST FEARLESS and inspiring women in African history was Queen Nzinga of the Ndongo and Matamba kingdoms. She lived in what is today the country of Angola. Read on to find out more about the many accomplishments of Queen Nzinga.

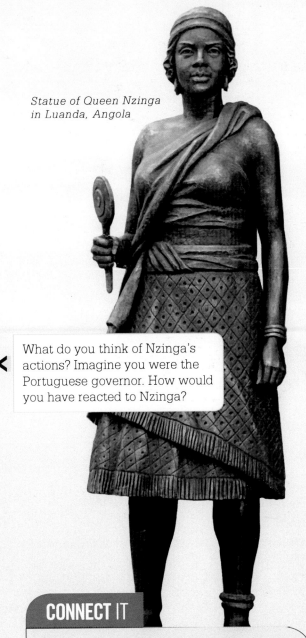

Statue of Queen Nzinga in Luanda, Angola

Queen Nzinga was born Nzinga Mbande around the early 1580s. During this time, the Portuguese were trying to colonize Central Africa. They built a settlement in the city of Luanda in order to gain control of that region and capture Africans to work in their mines and on their plantations. At the age of 39, Nzinga and her two sisters were asked by her brother King Ngola Mbande to meet with the Portuguese governor to negotiate a peace deal. At the meeting, the governor provided a mat for Nzinga to sit on, while he sat in a chair. Seeing this, Nzinga called one of her women-in-waiting to get down on her hands and knees and act as a chair for her to sit. By this action, she was telling the governor that she was his equal.

Nzinga became queen when her brother died suddenly. One year after becoming queen, in approximately 1627, she led her army in a 30-year war against the Portuguese. She also formed an alliance with the Dutch, allowing her to defeat the Portuguese army in 1647. Unfortunately, the Portuguese defeated the Dutch a year later.

Nzinga never gave up. Even in her sixties, she led armies into battle against the Portuguese. Despite attempts to capture or kill her, Queen Nzinga died peacefully in her eighties in 1663.

colonize: *gain control of another country*

What do you think of Nzinga's actions? Imagine you were the Portuguese governor. How would you have reacted to Nzinga?

CONNECT IT

The legacy of strong African women that Nzinga represents lives on today. Research a modern African woman who is making a difference in the world. Write a short report about her accomplishments.

TORTOISE and BABOON

THINK ABOUT IT

What is a story you would pass down to another generation? Tell a classmate why you think your story would be important for future generations to know.

MANY CULTURES HAVE traditional stories. Often, these stories are passed down through generations. This keeps cultures and traditions alive.

The tortoise is a common character in many African stories. He is often shown to be very smart. Even though he is slow, he shouldn't be underestimated. In this traditional folk tale from the Bantu people, we will see what happens when the crafty baboon tries to trick the clever tortoise.

One day close to suppertime, Tortoise was on his way home, inching slowly along at his usual pace. Baboon, who was up in a tree, spotted him and swooped down to greet him.

"Hello, Tortoise," said Baboon. "On your way home to eat supper?" he asked.

"No," replied Tortoise. "I didn't find much to eat today, unfortunately."

Baboon chuckled to himself. He had an idea.

"You are welcome to come to my place for supper. I have a nice pot already prepared," Baboon offered.

Tortoise was relieved. "That is very generous of you. I will take you up on your invitation," he said.

"Okay, follow me," said Baboon as he skipped gaily along the path toward home.

gaily: *happily; cheerfully*

Tortoise was not as fast as Baboon. In fact, he was very slow indeed. He crawled more slowly when he had to climb uphill or if the ground became bumpy. However, he did not become disheartened. What kept him going was the feast he was sure he would enjoy at Baboon's house.

Finally, Tortoise reached the place in the bush that Baboon called his home. Of course, Baboon had already arrived.

"There you are, Tortoise. I thought you would never get here," he said from the top of a tree branch.

Tortoise ignored Baboon's remark. He could smell food, and his pangs of hunger spoke louder than Baboon's rudeness. But Baboon was not done pulling Tortoise's leg.

He could smell food, and his pangs of hunger spoke louder than Baboon's rudeness.

"Supper is ready. You just have to climb up to the top of this tree, and you will have a wonderful feast," he called from his perch on the branches. "To start, I have made some nice, cold fruit juice."

Tortoise peered up into the tree branches, spotted the pots, and knew he would not be able to reach them. "Would you be so kind as to bring them down here?" he asked as politely as he could.

But Baboon was unsympathetic. "You must climb up here to enjoy supper with me," he said, laughing at his own joke.

Tortoise was disappointed and very angry. He was forced to turn around and march slowly back to his home with an empty stomach.

---

disheartened: *discouraged*

In this story, Baboon thinks tricking his friend is funny. Do you think tricking a friend can ever be funny? Why or why not?

This was not the end of the story. A week later, Baboon received an invitation to dine with Tortoise. He wondered if it was a trick like the one he had just pulled on Tortoise. Upon reflection, he decided that his friend was too good-natured to bear him any malice. He set out for Tortoise's home in the hope of a delicious meal.

It was the dry season across the land. Many brush fires had burned and scorched the earth, and the fields near Tortoise's home were blackened with soot. As Baboon approached his destination, Tortoise was waiting for him with the most delicious-smelling pot of food you could imagine.

"How are you, my friend?" asked Tortoise as Baboon approached.

"I'm just fine, and the smell of your supper is making me very hungry," Baboon replied.

"Before you eat, you will have to wash your hands. They are covered with soot and grime," said Tortoise. "Run back to the river and wash up. Then, we can sit down and eat."

malice: *bad feelings or grudges*

Baboon did just that. He bounded across the field to clean himself off in the river after his journey. However, upon his return, his hands and feet were as black as ever because he had crossed the same burnt fields as before.

"Are you kidding, Baboon?" said Tortoise. "Your hands are as dirty as they were before. You will have to go and clean them again before you sit down with me. I've already started my supper, so you better hurry up!" And with that, Tortoise began feasting on his food.

Try as he might, Baboon could not get his hands clean enough to have supper. Every time he crossed the fields, his hands became filthy again. As for Tortoise, he was quickly finishing the delicious meal he had prepared.

Do you think it is ever okay to play a trick on someone just because he or she has played a trick on you? Why or why not?

Try as he might, Baboon could not get his hands clean enough to have supper.

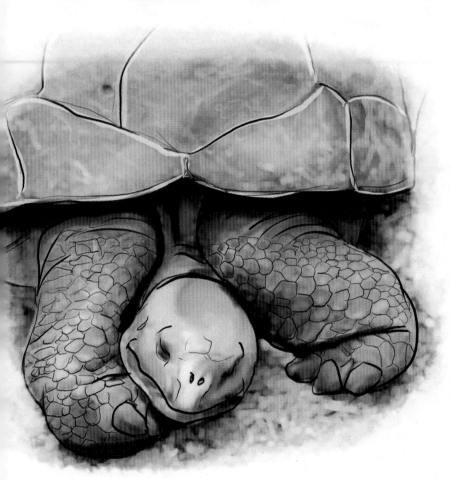

Finally, the food was finished, and Baboon realized that he would not be eating supper with Tortoise. Tortoise had indeed tricked him. He scurried back to his house in anger and embarrassment. Meanwhile, Tortoise withdrew into his shell with his belly full and a look of contentment on his face.

That will teach you to play tricks on your friends, dear Baboon, he thought. *You have gotten a taste of your own medicine.* And he drifted off to sleep for a long night's rest.

CONNECT IT

Research other traditional African stories that feature a tortoise. Compare and contrast the two stories. Based on your findings, do you think the tortoise behaves fairly? Why or why not? Discuss your thoughts in a small group.

ETHIOPIA:
A MARVEL OF THE ANCIENT WORLD

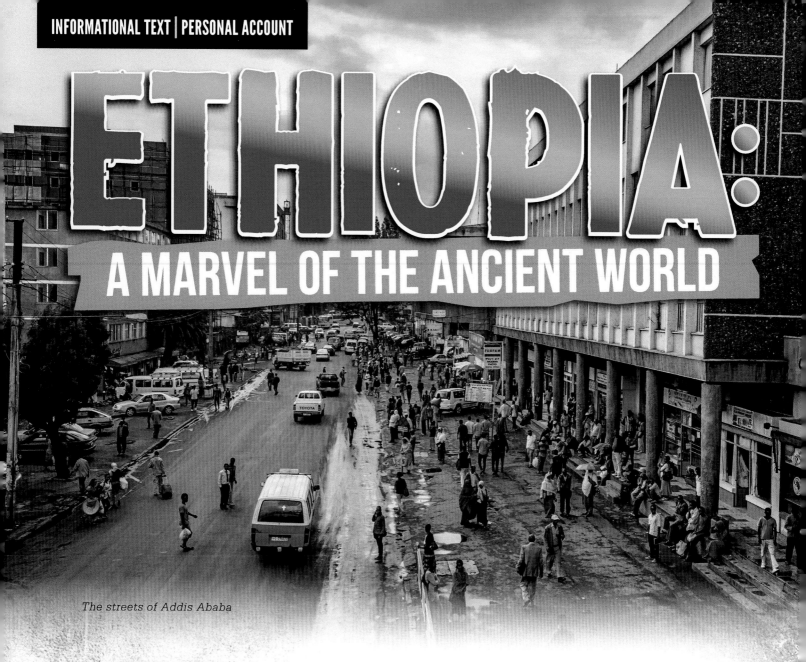

The streets of Addis Ababa

HABIBA COOPER DIALLO, selected among the "Top 20 Under 20" young Canadians in 2013, was only 16 years old when she started the Women's Health Organization International (WHOI) in April 2012. Her work has brought attention to African women's health care. Read her travel journal to learn about the ancient wonders she discovered in Ethiopia. The trip to Ethiopia inspired her to start WHOI.

ADDIS ABABA

Translated, *azmari bets* means "house of azmari." An *azmari* is an Ethiopian singer and musician.

We arrived in Bole on that 14th of December day. Bole is a suburb of Addis Ababa, the capital city. Ethiopia was awaiting our arrival. We were quickly introduced to the country's hidden treasures. Addis was a blast. At night, the upbeat and enticing sounds of *masenqo* and *washint* lured us into *azmari bets*, or nightclubs, like Yod Abyssinia.

masenqo: single-stringed lute or small guitar from Ethiopia and Eritrea
washint: wooden flute native to the Amhara people of Ethiopia

20

During the day, the city's hot, vibrant energy had us in the midst of vigorous *eskista* at Mesqel Square, or buying more *netelas* at Shiromeda, a market in Addis Ababa. After a few days, we headed south to a city called Shashamane. Then we went north to Gojjam, Gondar, Aksum, and Lalibela!

Addis Ababa, Ethiopia's capital, is home to many ancient sites. Mount Entoto — a mountain overlooking the city — is where Emperor Menelik II and Empress Taytu Betul built their palace when they founded Addis in 1886. The palace grounds also include a church and a modern museum containing several historic and religious artifacts.

About half an hour from Entoto are the Finfine hot springs, where Empress Taytu would frequently take mineral baths.

Ciao, Addis. Next stop: the Northern Highlands.

GOJJAM

Gojjam, a former kingdom in northwestern Ethiopia, lays claim to the famous city of Bahir Dar, where fertile soil spills into Lake Tana, the source of the magnificent Blue Nile River.

---

eskista: Ethiopian dance
netelas: handmade cloths, often worn to church

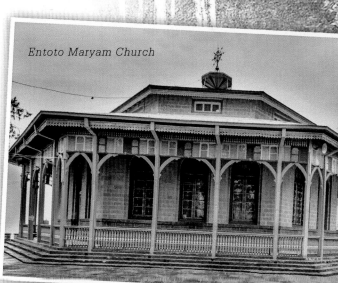

Entoto Maryam Church

Habiba Cooper Diallo, wearing a netela, climbing up the mountain to cross the Blue Nile Gorge

A monk reading in an Ethiopian monastery

When I arrived in Bahir Dar, my body was abuzz. My face tingled, and then I realized it was because I was over 1800 metres above sea level. The Ethiopian Highlands, which include Bahir Dar, are at an extremely high terrain. Bahir Dar means "seashore" in Amharic, the national language of Ethiopia. In addition to Lake Tana, Bahir Dar is home to many island monasteries, such as Kibran Gabriel, which was founded in the 14th century, and Daga Estifanos. At these monasteries, monks and nuns spend their days reading religious texts, painting, and preserving artifacts that date back to the 14th century.

Upon visiting the Nile, I climbed midway up a mountain overlooking the Blue Nile Gorge and then crossed a bridge onto a vast plateau. The sun was setting on the mountain, a most beautiful sight indeed. I was stunned to find a plateau at such an incredibly high height. There, villagers were up and about, cooking, and grazing their cows. *Ciao*, Gojjam. Next stop: the city of Aksum (or Axum), in the region of Tigray.

AKSUM

Once in Aksum, I was teleported back in time. The palace of the Queen of Sheba, the tomb of King Ezana, and the spectacular stelae at Northern Stelae Park are remnants of the ancient kingdom of Aksum that flourished between 100 and 940 CE.

Negash is a community in the eastern part of Tigray in a district called Wukro. The community has a very important history because it was the first Islamic settlement in Ethiopia. It was established in the 7th century when the Prophet Muhammad and his companions fled to Tigray due to violent threats they had received in Arabia. The Prophet and his companions built a mosque in the settlement, which can still be found there today.

LALIBELA

A few hours south of Negash is the fascinating town of Lalibela in the Amhara Region. The town is surrounded by a chain of immense, rugged mountains and is home to the world's largest stone structures. The city boasts 11 churches that were built from red volcanic rock. The church of Medhane Alem is the world's largest rock-hewn church. It measures 11.5 metres tall, and has an area of about 800 square metres. The most famous of Lalibela's churches, Bet Giyorgis, was carved in the form of a cross and is said to have been built with the help of angels. Bet Giyorgis means "house or church of Saint George." Many people call Bet Giyorgis the Eighth Wonder of the World because of its complex structure and design.

Today, many parts of Ethiopia are bustling metropolitan centres. However, the antiquity of the country can be felt all throughout at the monasteries of Lake Tana, the Aksumite obelisks, the mosque of Negash, and Entoto Maryam Church in Addis Ababa.

Addis Ababa, the Northern Highlands, Aksum, and Lalibela. Thanks to these historical sites, Ethiopia's history will continue to live on for many years to come.

antiquity: *ancient past; great age*

Medhane Alem Church

Bet Giyorgis

Obelisk in the kingdom of Aksum

CONNECT IT

Choose one place that Habiba Cooper Diallo mentions in her travel journal. Conduct your own research to learn more about it. In the voice of an excited tourist, write a postcard to a friend or family member about this place.

MANSA MUSA I:
THE RICHEST MAN WHO EVER LIVED

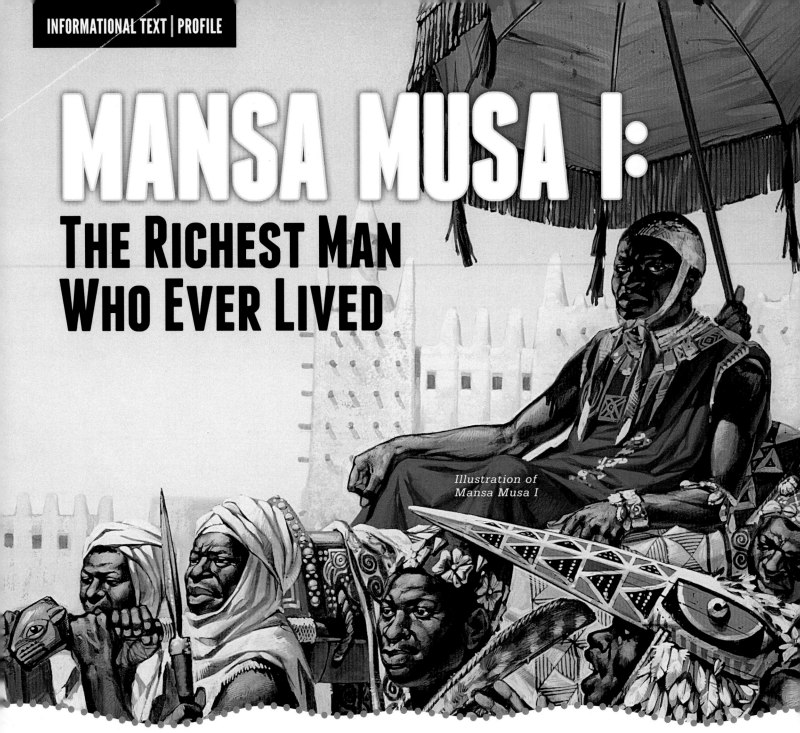

Illustration of Mansa Musa I

READ THIS PROFILE to learn about Mansa Musa I, the richest man of all time.

Did you know that the richest man in history was from Africa? His name was Mansa Musa I, and he ruled the kingdom of Mali from 1312 CE until his death around 1337 CE. According to the website *Celebrity Net Worth*, Musa's fortune amounted to $400 billion when adjusted to today's prices. He was worth three times as much as Microsoft founder Bill Gates! In fact, Musa topped the list of the 25 wealthiest people of all time.

Little is known of the early life of Musa. He was the great-nephew of the warrior king Sundiata Keita. It was Sundiata who first established Mali as a major empire in the 13th century. In about 1312, Musa came to power. At that time, Mali had millions of people spread across a vast territory. Ancient Mali included parts of modern-day Mali, Mauritania, Guinea, Senegal, and Burkina Faso, as well as other countries.

GOVERNING THE KINGDOM

The king's empire united many populations. These populations included farmers from the Atlantic coast, nomads from the Sahara Desert, and farmers and traders from many other regions. Trade routes criss-crossed the empire, exchanging salt and fabrics for ivory and gold.

Mali was divided into 12 provinces, each run by a governor reporting to Musa. However, Musa controlled trade, farming, and business for the entire kingdom with help from advisers. One adviser was in charge of the empire's money. Another made agreements with people in other countries. Other officials looked after farming, fishing, and working in the forests. An army of 100 000 men were stationed across the empire. The army made sure it was as safe as possible for travellers and traders who journeyed throughout Mali.

◀ Why would Musa choose to unite several populations?

JOURNEY TO MECCA

Musa was a devout Muslim. A Muslim is a person who practises the religion of Islam. Islamic law requires that all faithful Muslims make a *hajj*, or holy visit, at least once in their lifetime to Mecca, the city where Islam started. Musa made a famous pilgrimage to Mecca in 1324.

The number of people who travelled with the king was the size of a small city. Some reports said there were 10 000 soldiers, 60 000 porters, and many teachers, doctors, lawyers, griots, and other officials and relatives.

Musa's journey through the Egyptian capital of Cairo was legendary. Some historians believe that Musa's caravan carried as much as two tonnes of gold. In fact, Musa brought and gave away so much gold that it is said the global price of gold dropped significantly for over 10 years. This is the only time in recorded history that one man directly influenced the price of gold in the Mediterranean.

devout: *very religious*
porters: *people who carry things for others*
griots: *storytellers*

Today, more than 15 million Muslims visit Mecca each year.

ART AND LEARNING

On his way back through Cairo after his visit to Mecca, Musa asked a well-known architect named Abu Es Haq Es Saheli to join his court. Es Saheli built mosques in the cities of Gao, Djenné, and Timbuktu. Es Saheli's structures were large rectangular buildings made of mud brick with wooden branches sticking out. The branches helped hold the building together. The mosques were well suited to the hot climate. The buildings remained cool inside even when the temperature went up to 43 degrees Celsius. Es Saheli also built new palaces for the king.

Musa himself read and wrote in Arabic, and he encouraged learning and culture during his reign. He built many schools and libraries throughout the kingdom, and sent scholars to study in the great schools and universities of Morocco. Musa encouraged Malians to write legal papers, religious literature, and poetry in Arabic. Djenné and Timbuktu became centres of learning that attracted scholars and students from all over Africa and the Middle East. Under Musa's reign, more and more Malians learned to read and write. Artists were also important to Musa. Musicians, dancers, poets, and storytellers performed all over Mali.

> Why do you think a ruler would want to encourage learning in his kingdom?

The Great Mosque of Djenné

HISTORICAL IMPORTANCE

Mali became prosperous and peaceful during Musa's rule. Musa put Mali on the map in more ways than one. People from around the world spoke of his trip to the Middle East for many years to come. In 1375, Musa was pictured on a Spanish map, the Catalan Atlas, along with the huge territory of his empire. On the map, Musa wears a golden crown and holds a large golden nugget in one hand and a golden staff in the other, symbolizing his great wealth. The Catalan Atlas can still be viewed today in the British Museum.

prosperous: *wealthy; flourishing*

Detail of the Catalan Atlas featuring Mansa Musa

TIMBUKTU

Founded around 1100 CE, this ancient city became the cultural and commercial centre of West Africa. Its university, Sankore, was famous throughout the Muslim world. Today, Timbuktu is a city of around 54 000 people and has beautiful mosques and buildings. Many of these structures are protected as UNESCO World Heritage sites.

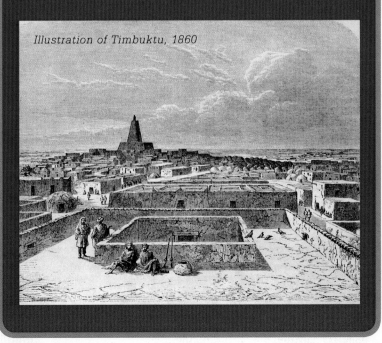

Illustration of Timbuktu, 1860

CONNECT IT

What are some qualities that you think a good leader should have? Does Mansa Musa have these qualities? How do people benefit from having a good leader?

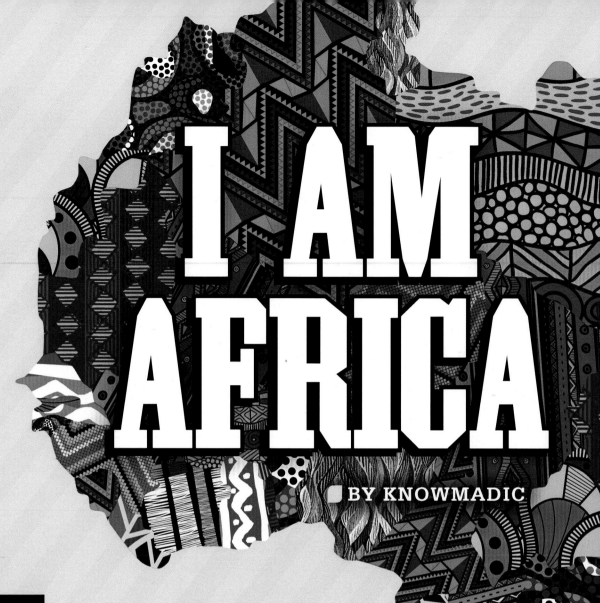

I AM AFRICA

BY KNOWMADIC

THINK ABOUT IT

How might an artist's heritage or culture influence his or her art? Share your ideas with a partner.

READ THIS POEM to learn about the connection Ahmed "Knowmadic" Ali has to his African heritage.

ABOUT THE POET

Ahmed Ali, also known as Knowmadic, is a Somali Canadian poet who lives in Edmonton, Alberta. He tours all over Canada and the United States, entertaining audiences with his poems. He was recently named one of the Alberta Council for Global Cooperation's Top 30 Under 30. In 2013, he received the Edmonton Arts Council's Cultural Diversity in the Arts Award.

These veins run blood from Africa,
I was born in Africa
I was fed Africa
then I was torn from Africa
parents fed up with Africa
so we fled Africa

Landed in a land far, far from Africa
and we have long since forgotten
that we are not from Africa
we are Africa

Remember, we come from a land
where we are kings and queens
where the trees
use their vines and leaves as rosary,
there are water beds
imbedded with the essence of life
and while the heavy-eyed count sheep
the dormant souls of our ancestors
resting in the Atlantic
are carried in river beds back home.
They say that imitation is
the greatest form of flattery
then would it not be vein
for us to take our customs back
since we put the art in artery

There is no reason to
go searching for my history
In hidden caves or baked clay buried deep
it's visible on my face
the way I carry myself
The proverbs of our people
the scarification on the
foreheads of Sudanese tribes

the shapes of our women's
bodies who mimic
all of the geographical
differences of Africa
and the colourful cloth
Like a rainbow bending
backwards to tie their beauty together.

I swear god must have etched
my being into its core
because my soul is drawn to Africa
I long for the days I can
sit back and overdose
on Africa

---

rosary: *string of beads used in religious prayer; rose garden or bed of roses*
imbedded: *enclosed tightly; fixed firmly*
dormant: *asleep; inactive*
scarification: *marks or small cuts*
mimic: *copy*

Many have fallen into
the trap of asking me
if I am from Africa
I say hush,
I am Africa

Don't tell me what you have read
because I am a manuscript
written in African
So read my lips
and my body language
and if you are ever confused
ask for translation
because I don't understand
how you might misinterpret
bare feet kissing ground
as barbaric
pass my oral tradition
as a mere clicking of tongues

Where I am from, wisdom drips
from the beards of the elders
and knowledge rests between their lips
ready to create revolutions
and their philosophies
are always willing to back them up
so I could care little
about what you've been told
because we all know well enough
that only shepherds should rely on what they heard

where I am from
bloodlines are borders
neighbours are relatives
tribes are families
Africa is within us and
with us therefore
I am 56 nations in 1
and my mother is known
as the cradle of life

I am not from Africa

I AM AFRICA!

_____

manuscript: *original copy of a piece of writing before it is printed*

CONNECT IT

With a partner, discuss how a person's heritage can shape his or her identity. Write a short paragraph explaining your culture and why it is important to you.

Trip of a Lifetime

THINK ABOUT IT

If you were to write a story about ancient Africa, what would your story be about?

IN THIS SHORT STORY, read about how the ancient ruins of Zimbabwe captured a boy's attention hundreds of years after they were made.

Jamal was bored and restless. As the bus drove farther and farther away from the city, it felt like he was travelling back in time. The paved boulevards, shops, and tall shiny buildings of the city gave way to countryside, farms, dirt roads, and bush. The bus passed small villages with animals grazing nearby. Women walked alongside the roads with huge piles of sticks or large containers on their heads. It was scorching hot outside, but at least the bus was air-conditioned.

Jamal, his parents, and his sister, Denise, were on a month-long vacation in Africa. They had first jetted to Johannesburg in South Africa. Then, they made their way to Pretoria, one of the capital cities of South Africa.

Jamal's family then flew to Harare, the capital of Zimbabwe, which got its name from the Great Zimbabwe civilization that they would soon visit, after the long bus ride was finished.

"This will be the trip of a lifetime," Dad had said about their trip to Africa, but Jamal wasn't so sure. So far, he hadn't seen any big animals like lions, cheetahs, rhinos, or elephants. What was the point of going to see some old buildings that nobody lived in anymore? It didn't sound like much fun to him.

Why do you think Jamal felt this way? If you were on a vacation in Zimbabwe, would you feel the same way?

31

All of a sudden, the bus jerked to a halt.

A herd of goats had started to cross the road, and they were preventing the bus from passing. The driver honked furiously at them for several minutes. Finally, the goats moved off the road, and the bus roared its engine and started rolling again. Jamal sighed. Surely, they'd see something more interesting than a herd of goats.

Hours and hours passed. At last, the bus pulled up to the gates of an inviting-looking compound called the Great Zimbabwe Hotel. They had arrived at their destination, and it was none too soon!

Bright and early the next morning, everyone gathered in the hotel lobby. While waiting for the walking tour to depart, Jamal made friends with a boy named Yohann, who was visiting from Germany with his parents. The boys played tag, zigzagging between the other tourists, until a tour guide entered the lobby.

"Follow me," said the guide, leading the tourists along a long path.

Jamal knew that they were going to see the ruins of Great Zimbabwe. His sister, Denise, was studying archaeology at a university back in Canada. She couldn't wait to visit the site. Jamal, of course, was less enthusiastic.

The first stop on the tour was the Great Enclosure. The guide explained that this was likely the home of the royal family, their courtiers, and officials.

"Great Zimbabwe was the capital of a vast ancient trading empire that covered much of modern-day Zimbabwe and parts of Mozambique. It existed from 1200 to 1500 CE. It stretched from southern Africa to the Swahili coast of East Africa. From there, it reached as far away as Arabia, India, and China. The Zimbabweans traded gold and ivory for things such as beads, bracelets, porcelain, and glass."

Jamal wasn't really listening to the tour guide. He had spotted several monkeys that were screeching with laughter and swinging from branch to branch in a nearby tree.

"Yohann! Come here!" he cried, pointing upward toward the trees. His new friend joined him, and the pair jumped around, mimicking the monkeys in the tree.

"The Great Enclosure is the remains of the palace where the royal family lived," the guide continued. "As you can see, these walls are quite huge and measure 11 metres in height. You will also notice that there is nothing gluing these bricks together, just amazing precision and craftsmanship. More than one million bricks were used to build these walls. It's quite a stunning feat of architecture."

The group entered the palace enclosure. They could see more walls within walls, with some very narrow corridors leading to other parts of the enclosure. Jamal's curiosity was piqued. They looked like secret passageways. He wanted to find out more! When the guide's back was turned, Jamal looked at Yohann and Yohann looked at Jamal. It was clear they had the same idea.

How do you think the people of ancient Zimbabwe made their bricks fit so well without anything holding them together?

---

precision: *accuracy; exactness*

"Let's go!" said Yohann in a loud whisper.

Jamal's parents didn't notice when the boys slowly edged toward a passageway. As they entered the opening, they became completely surrounded by stone walls, which towered almost 10 metres above them. The passage curved around and around at some length, until they found themselves in a courtyard. Finally, Jamal had found his exciting adventure.

Yohann and Jamal spotted a huge cone-shaped stone tower made of the same bricks without mortar, just like the other walls. It appeared to be open at the top.

Finally, Jamal had found his exciting adventure.

"I wonder what's inside there," Yohann whispered slowly.

"There's only one way to find out," Jamal whispered.

As the boys moved toward the cone formation, something shiny on the ground caught Jamal's eye. He moved closer to see what it could be. Buried almost completely in the earth was something gold. He fell to his knees and examined the object closely, using his hands to brush away the dirt.

"It's a gold ring," Jamal exclaimed.

"It must have belonged to the king of Great Zimbabwe," said Yohann.

"Who else could it belong to? This was his palace," Jamal replied confidently.

As Jamal examined the ring thoroughly, he found an inscription in a lettering he did not understand. Could this be the language they had spoken in Great Zimbabwe?

Jamal slipped the ring into his pocket. How great would it be to come away from this trip with actual golden treasure that he had discovered himself? Jamal imagined he could sell the ring to a museum for thousands, maybe millions, of dollars!

As the boys stood up to continue their adventure, they suddenly realized they weren't alone.

"Where do you think you're going?" asked a stern security guard, who immediately marched them back to the other tourists.

"Did you boys have an interesting adventure?" the tour guide asked with a twinkle in his eye.

Dad gave Jamal an angry glare. Jamal knew he had better stick with his family from here on out.

---

mortar: *substance that holds bricks together and makes structures stronger*

The tour guide picked up where he left off. "Among the interesting items that have been discovered on this site is a 14th-century copper coin that comes from the east coast of Africa. Of course, much of the gold that was owned by the king was stolen by explorers and treasure hunters in the 1800s and early 1900s. This is an important part of our heritage that has been taken from us and future generations."

A wave of guilt overcame Jamal.

"Sir …," he volunteered timidly. "I have something to show you. Yohann and I found this." Jamal pulled the ring from his pocket. "We think it belonged to a king. Maybe it should remain here for the people of Zimbabwe."

"It is so kind of you to return to us this treasure of the king," the guide said with great appreciation. He chose not to mention that it looked suspiciously similar to the wedding band that his assistant had lost over a year ago.

The group made their way across the plain to the Hill Complex. Stone steps led to another ancient passageway. It became steeper and narrower the higher they climbed.

"These buildings were built earlier than those of the Great Enclosure complex and have been dated to 900 years old. We believe this was the site of a royal city, as well as a religious centre," the tour guide continued.

The group assembled at the top of the hill. They could see the same brick construction as earlier, but also huge granite rocks, which formed some sort of monument. It was thrilling, and the view from the top of the hill was amazing. Jamal and Yohann imagined themselves wielding royal power and influence from on high.

"I'm the king of the woooorrrrlllld …!" Jamal shouted gleefully from the summit.

His voice echoed across the plateau. It was obvious why the tour guide said that these were the largest ancient structures south of the Sahara Desert. They were quite a spectacular sight, full of wonder and mystery.

After the tour concluded, Mom bought Jamal and Denise each a beautiful soapstone bird, the national symbol of Zimbabwe today. They were replicas of the large bird sculptures found on the Hill Complex. Dad was right. This had been the trip of a lifetime. Jamal was thankful that he was there.

> "Among the interesting items that have been discovered on this site is a 14th-century copper coin that comes from the east coast of Africa."

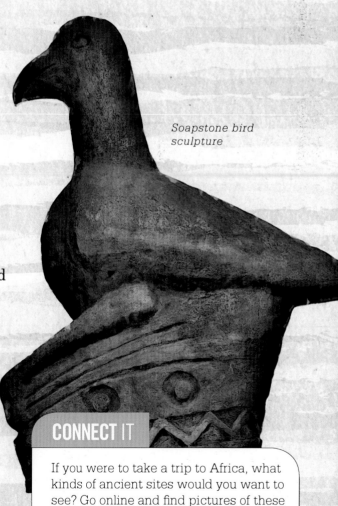

Soapstone bird sculpture

CONNECT IT

If you were to take a trip to Africa, what kinds of ancient sites would you want to see? Go online and find pictures of these ancient sites. Tell your class why you would like to visit them.

MATH AND WRITING IN EARLY AFRICA

THINK ABOUT IT

What do you know about African inventions? Why might many African inventions be unknown?

AFRICA IS HOME to the world's earliest math and writing systems. Read this report to find out how the early people of Africa helped lead the way to present-day math and writing.

MATH IN EARLY AFRICA

Africa holds some of the oldest examples of mathematical tools and ideas. Read on to see some of Africa's oldest mathematical treasures.

THE LEBOMBO BONE (35 000 BCE)

This baboon fibula, or shinbone, has been called the world's oldest mathematical tool. The bone was found in the Lebombo Mountains in Swaziland in the 1970s. The bone has 29 marks. The use for this bone has been widely debated. Some say it could simply be a tally stick, while others say it could have been used as a lunar calendar. Interestingly, the baboon was a symbol for the moon, math, and time in early African societies. Some researchers say the Lebombo Bone looks like the calendar sticks used by Bushmen clans in Namibia today.

lunar: *related to the phases of the moon*

ZIMBABWE

BOTSWANA

MOZAMBIQUE

Limpopo

Lebombo Mountains

SWAZILAND

SOUTH AFRICA

LESOTHO

An illustration of the Lebombo Bone showing the markings

THE ISHANGO BONE (20 000 BCE)

Belgian explorers found this bone in 1960 in the present-day Democratic Republic of the Congo. Just like the Lebombo Bone, the Ishango Bone is a baboon's fibula. The Ishango Bone has three columns of markings adding up to 60, 48, and 60. Some researchers say the number of markings may have been used to solve simple math problems. Others say that the Ishango Bone could be a calendar, just like the Lebombo Bone. The Ishango Bone can be seen at the Royal Belgian Institute of Natural Sciences in Belgium.

The Ishango Bone

RHIND MATHEMATICAL PAPYRUS (1650 BCE)

The Rhind Mathematical Papyrus

This text was found in Thebes, Egypt, and was purchased by Alexander Henry Rhind in 1858. The papyrus is named after Rhind. The Rhind Mathematical Papyrus is a copy of an older papyrus dated between 1985 and 1795 BCE, but that papyrus has never been found. The Rhind Mathematical Papyrus has three parts with many math problems, including multiplication, fractions, and algebra. These math problems would have been helpful in building the pyramids in Egypt.

papyrus: *handmade writing material used in ancient times*

TIMBUKTU MATHEMATICAL MANUSCRIPTS (1200S CE)

These manuscripts are just a few of the hundreds of thousands of manuscripts in Timbuktu, Mali, in West Africa. At one of the world's oldest universities, Sankore, many Timbuktu manuscripts contain complicated mathematical and scientific problems. Many also deal with astronomy. In ancient times, Timbuktu was known as a place where many scholars would meet. These manuscripts show that difficult mathematical problems were being understood in Africa much earlier than previously thought.

A page from the Timbuktu Mathematical Manuscripts

WRITING IN EARLY AFRICA

Early African writing is one of the oldest forms of writing. In some cases, African writing is older than ancient Greek and Asian writing. Here are some examples of some of Africa's oldest writing systems.

NSIBIDI (5000 BCE TO PRESENT)

MEETING   REFLECTION   TREK

JOURNEY   LOVE

Many people in West Africa used this ancient writing, most often from present-day Nigeria and Cameroon. Nsibidi uses symbols and pictures to represent ideas, much like Egyptian hieroglyphs. In fact, Egyptian hieroglyphs and Nsibidi share many of the same symbols. Later versions of Nsibidi can be found in the early languages of Cuba and Haiti. Some researchers believe Nsibidi dates back to almost 5000 BCE, but this is still widely debated.

EGYPTIAN HIEROGLYPHS (3200 BCE TO 400 CE)

Hieroglyphs are symbols or pictures used to represent words, syllables, or sounds. Early hieroglyphs have been found on pottery dating from approximately 4000 BCE in Egypt, south of Giza. Hieroglyphs were written on papyrus and carved into stone. They were a mystery until the Rosetta Stone was discovered in 1799. This stone had the same text written three times: in Greek, in common hieroglyphs, and in official hieroglyphs. This allowed translators to crack the mystery of the Egyptian hieroglyphs. Egyptian hieroglyphs were the inspiration for many of the world's first alphabets.

VAI (3000 BCE OR 1800s CE TO PRESENT)

According to the Ta Neter Foundation, the Vai writing system was discovered in Mali and dates to approximately 3000 BCE. Others argue that a man in Liberia invented this writing system in the early 1800s after having a dream about the symbols. In this writing system, symbols are used to represent a consonant and a vowel. This kind of writing system is known as a syllable alphabet. According to the website *Ethnologue*, this writing system is still used by approximately 120 000 people in Sierra Leone and Liberia. This makes Vai one of the world's oldest writing systems still in use today.

DE   KPI

MGBC   BOH

ZA   KOH

GE'EZ (800 BCE TO PRESENT)

Just like Vai, the Ge'ez writing system uses a syllable alphabet. The oldest form of Ge'ez writing was found on a monument in Eritrea, near the Ethiopian border, dating back to approximately 800 BCE. Even though this writing was used mainly in churches, it was also used to write texts about history, medicine, and law. This writing system is still in use today in Ethiopia and nearby countries. It was also the inspiration for some modern languages in Ethiopia. Ge'ez is also used by some Ethiopians who have emigrated to other countries.

emigrated: *left a country to live in another*

CONNECT IT

Which example did you find the most interesting? With a partner, research another example of early African math or writing. Write a short paragraph about your example, and include any pictures you find.

Timbuktu Calligrapher Keeps Ancient Knowledge Alive

BY ROBYN DIXON
LOS ANGELES TIMES
23 APRIL 2013

THINK ABOUT IT

Read the title of this selection. In a small group, talk about the term "ancient knowledge." Why do you think it is important to pass knowledge down from generation to generation?

Boubacar Sadeck

IN APRIL 2012, Timbuktu experienced much violence after groups fought to control this ancient city. During the fighting, many ancient buildings and libraries were destroyed. The famous Ahmed Baba Institute of Higher Learning and Islamic Research, where many ancient manuscripts are held, was one site that was attacked.

But thanks to the work of the people of Timbuktu, many manuscripts have been saved. In this article, find out about one man's work to preserve the knowledge and history of these ancient texts.

Homemade twig pens stand like off-duty soldiers in a jar on Boubacar Sadeck's worktable. The morning sun steals into a room stuffed with a jumble of papers, ink bottles, and stretched animal hides. He sits thoughtfully before a blank sheet of paper, with several old manuscripts — the colour of dark tea and covered with Arabic script — open at his side. …

hides: *animal skins*

"My weakness, my love, is calligraphy," said the scribe, who fled Timbuktu, famed for its collection of centuries-old manuscripts, when Islamist militias invaded last year. "If I go a day without writing, I feel as if something is missing or strange. When I sit down with my paper and my pen, I feel wonderful. I feel at ease."

Copying and recopying old manuscripts is an ancient Timbuktu calling. In the 15th century, there were hundreds of scribes; the job was one of the most highly paid and prestigious occupations in the city. ...

Sadeck, at 38 the youngest of Timbuktu's copyists, doesn't earn much money from his craft. It's his sheer love of the liquid, graceful Arabic script and the meaning of the ancient words that keeps him working — now in Bamako, Mali's capital. ...

When he fled Timbuktu last April, he carried the family's collection of 80 manuscripts. Now he works in a small, bright studio. ...

calligraphy: *artistic handwriting*

> ◄ Why do you think scribes, or copiers, were considered prestigious and important?

Some of Sadeck's manuscripts and works

The militias were driven out of the northern cities by the French and Malian armies in January, but many fear it will be years before life returns to normal in Timbuktu.

[There are] doubts about when or even whether Timbuktu's collection of manuscripts, many thousands of which were smuggled out during the ... occupation, can return to its home in the city's Ahmed Baba Institute.

As Sadeck works in his studio, another small room in Bamako is crammed full with 31 large metal trunks. ...

Inside, manuscripts are neatly packed. ...

Mohammed Maiga, 33, a researcher at the institute, stands before the metal boxes. ... They hold a large portion of Ahmed Baba's collection.

After the arrival of the [militias], he and others loaded the manuscripts ... onto motorcycles and ferried them to private houses in Timbuktu. Maiga then loaded the manuscripts into the locked metal boxes and sent them by truck to Bamako. ...

The militants burned an unknown number of manuscripts before fleeing the city. ...

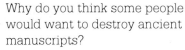

Why do you think some people would want to destroy ancient manuscripts?

Workers from the Ahmed Baba Centre for Documentation and Research go through burnt manuscripts.

Shamil Jeppie, head of the Timbuktu Manuscripts Project at South Africa's University of Cape Town, works with researchers from Ahmed Baba …

To Jeppie, the collection's real value lies in the ancient knowledge the manuscripts contain and the window they provide onto a golden age in the city. [Back then,] people shared knowledge by transcribing books, as they do these days by posting information on the Internet. "These are priceless because they can [explain] aspects of African history and world history."

The manuscripts cover centuries of Islamic [knowledge] on subjects that include religion, medicine, ethics, astronomy, trade, literature, and architecture. But mining nuggets of information about a distant past from them is painstaking work.

"The Arabic manuscripts are very hard to translate," Jeppie said. "It's West African Arabic script. It's not standard Arabic. It can be very depressing — it takes so long to work through a tiny section."

> The best way to preserve the manuscripts from termites and decay, he believes, is for their owners to touch them daily, use them, read them, and study them.

Centuries ago, scribes copied books that came to the city, creating the famous Timbuktu manuscripts. Sadeck's solitary work is one of the last echoes of what was then a great enterprise.

Sadeck took up the craft at the urging of his uncle, a well-known calligrapher, and became hooked. …

The best way to preserve the manuscripts from termites and decay, he believes, is for their owners to touch them daily, use them, read them, and study them.

"If they are packed away in the dark, termites can easily get them," he said. "If you keep your eyes on them, they survive."

What do you think Sadeck means when he says, "If you keep your eyes on them, they survive"?

transcribing: *copying*
enterprise: *project*

CONNECT IT

Why might it be important to preserve ancient writing? Make a list of reasons with a partner.

MARISHANA MABUSELA:
Interview With an
Archaeologist

THINK ABOUT IT

In what ways do archaeologists teach us about ancient civilizations?

MARISHANA MABUSELA IS living her dream. She works as an archaeological field technician. In this interview, she tells her mother, Adrienne Shadd, how the work she does helps others learn about ancient civilizations.

Marishana Mabusela in Wadi Rum, Jordan

Adrienne Shadd: What do archaeologists do?

Marishana Mabusela: Archaeologists study the human past. We analyze material from the past to learn more about people and their way of life. We use a variety of methods, such as surveying an area of land, excavating below the ground, and analyzing the material in a laboratory. From there, we can create interpretations based on our findings.

Archaeology is an interesting field that uses science, history, anthropology, art, language, and modern-day observations of people (called ethnographies) to tell us more about the people that came before us. These, as well as many other methods, give us a better understanding of the world around us and help us better understand the archaeological record.

surveying: *examining*
excavating: *digging carefully*
anthropology: *study of humans, especially their societies and customs*

AS: How did you become interested in archaeology as a field of study?

MM: I first became interested in archaeology in elementary school, in grade 5, when my teacher first taught the class about the ancient Mayan and Egyptian civilizations. I also used to watch movies and TV specials about archaeologists and paleontologists, studying fossils and going into the Great Pyramid of Giza in Egypt. Being an archaeologist seemed like such a cool thing to do, and it always seemed so exciting to me. I just never imagined I could become one!

It wasn't until university that I realized being an archaeologist was my destiny. When I was younger, I didn't always believe in myself because I didn't realize my true potential. When I figured out that this was what I wanted to do, I studied and worked as hard as I could, and I have never looked back.

AS: Is there a particular area in archaeology that you have focused on?

MM: Most archaeologists find an area of the world, a particular culture or group of people, or a time period that they are most interested in. Once they do, they end up studying that area for most of their life. I'm not quite at that point yet, and I am still figuring out what area of archaeology I love most, because truthfully, I love everything about archaeology! Every time I learn something new, I end up liking that, too.

So far, I have mainly studied Middle Eastern archaeology, and I have excavated twice in Jordan on a site with about 10 different layers of occupation, spanning thousands of years.

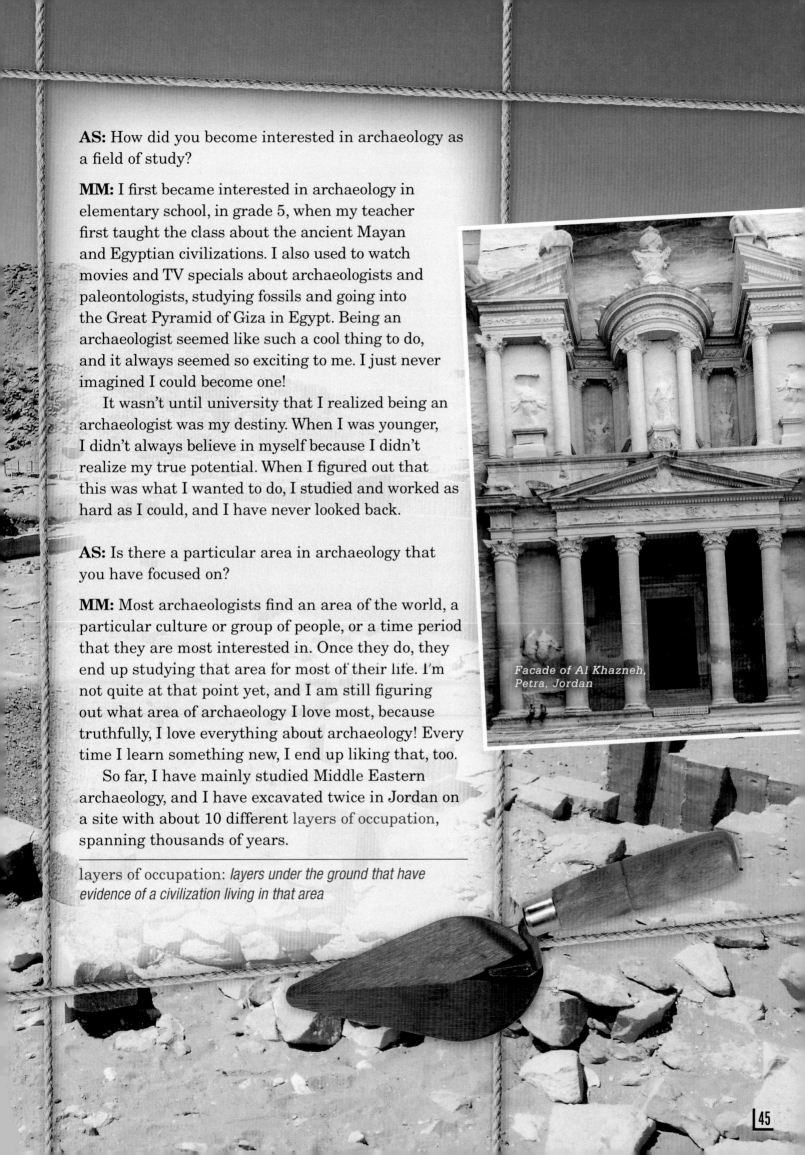

Facade of Al Khazneh, Petra, Jordan

layers of occupation: *layers under the ground that have evidence of a civilization living in that area*

45

AS: Tell me more about your work in Jordan. What did you do there?

MM: In Jordan, I worked at a field school, and we did excavations on a mound where (thousands of years before us) people from different time periods built on top of one another. Instead of tearing down old houses and walls like we do today, they used them to help build their own. For weeks, in the hot desert sun, we dug down very carefully and found a lot of artifacts that had been buried for thousands of years. It was amazing being one of the first people to find these objects after all that time underground. We also cleaned the artifacts, took notes, as well as analyzed and wrote reports based on what we found. It was the hardest I've ever worked, but it's also the happiest I've ever been.

AS: Tell me about living in Jordan.

MM: Jordan, halfway across the world in a Middle Eastern country, was unlike anywhere I've ever lived before. It was almost out of a movie, and I loved it. Every day was an adventure and a new experience. The food was good, the people were friendly, and the clothes and the language were different, but most of all, the scenery was absolutely beautiful. I felt like a true archaeologist in Jordan.

AS: Talk about your most recent work with Archaeological Services Inc. What does this company do and what is your role with the company?

Mabusela engaged in field excavation at the Tell Madaba Archaeological Project in Jordan.

MM: Archaeological Services Inc. is a company that seeks to preserve and protect Ontario's heritage. At this company, I am an "archaeological technician," which means that I work outside every day just north of Toronto. We survey and excavate archaeological material in areas that need to be checked before a house, building, or road is built. What we do is look for material, and once we find it, we excavate and collect it, saving it from being destroyed by construction. We mainly work on Native villages and early Euro-Canadian sites.

One of the many things found surveying in southern Ontario with Archaeological Services Inc.

AS: Do you want to continue your studies in archaeology? Do you think you might want to work in Africa on an ancient site there?

MM: Even though I don't have a specific area of archaeology that I want to study, I know that I definitely want to continue my education. I want to continue learning so that I can find something I love, and I think deep down, it is African archaeology. I have always been interested in travelling around Africa, and I love the history of the continent and of the different people, cultures, languages, and ancient sites that exist there. I would love to go on an excavation in Africa … It has been one of my dreams.

AS: Have you travelled in Africa before?

MM: I've been to South Africa before — where my father's side of the family lives — and it was a beautiful place. I'd love to go back, as well as travel to many other countries. …

AS: What advice would you give to young people who want to become archaeologists?

MM: Follow your dreams. Go to school, learn as much as you can, and fill your soul with the wonders archaeology has to offer. All you need is passion to succeed. When you're doing something you're passionate about, it doesn't feel like work. Stick with it. You never know what you'll find.

CONNECT IT

Imagine you are an archaeologist working at an ancient African site. Write a short journal entry about your experiences.

Index

Acknowledgements

Ali, Ahmed. "I Am Africa." © Ahmed Ali. Reprinted with permission of the author.

Dixon, Robyn. "Timbuktu calligrapher keeps ancient learning alive," from *Los Angeles Times*, 23 April 2013. Copyright © *Los Angeles Times* 2013. All rights reserved.

Photo Sources
Cover: Pyramid of Meroe–Robert Harding/Glowimages.com; **4:** [soil–Korionov; big stone–J.Schelkle; trowel–Tischenko Irina] Shutterstock.com; border–Megan Little; **5:** [brush–homydesign; hand–photka; stone–J.Schelkle; shovel–harmpeti] Shutterstock.com; **6:** [sand texture–llaszlo; grass texture–llaszlo; skull–Creativemarc; crops–bloodsugar; hieroglyphics–Fedor Selivanov] Shutterstock.com; sphnynx–Jon Bodsworth; illustrations–Megan Little; **7:** [gold–Eli Maier; stela–Anton_Ivanov] Shutterstock.com; metal tools–Goethe University Frankfurt/Nicole Rupp; bust–Werner Forman Archive/Glowimages.com; **8:** [salt–aperturesound] Shutterstock.com; Kanembu warriors–NYPLDigitalGallery; Ife head–British Museum; Great Enclosure–Jan Derk; **9:** [frame–Dario Sabljak; ship–John Copland] Shutterstock.com; Mansa Musa–Abraham Cresques of Mallorca; Queen Nzinga statue–Erik Cleves Kristensen; **10:** [waves–emart; woven pattern–hax; Africa–michal812] Shutterstock.com; **11:** hieroglyphics–DeAgostini/Superstock; **12:** [texture–Lucy Baldwin; hieroglyphs–Fedor Selivanov] Shutterstock.com; model–Andreas Praefcke; **13:** seeds–Sinan Niyazi KUTSAL/Shutterstock.com; Hatshepsut bust–Rob Koopman; cosmetics–Science and Society/Science and Society/Superstock; **14:** background–Apostrophe/Shutterstock.com; Nubian archers–Universal Images Group/Superstock; Meroe pyramids–Wufei07; iron grooming kit–courtesy of the Oriental Institute of the University of Chicago; **15:** landscape–EcoPrint/Shutterstock.com; statue–Damianne R President; **16:** illustrations–Cheeky Designs; **20:** [background–Ensuper; Addis Ababa–milosk50] Shutterstock.com; **21:** Entoto Maryam–Dereje/Shutterstock.com; Habiba C. Diallo–courtesy of Habiba C. Diallo; **22:** monk–Superstock/Glowimages.com; **23:** Medhane Alem–Clive Chilvers/ Shutterstock.com; Bet Giyorgis–Bernard Gagnon; obelisk–iStockphoto.com/ © Meinzahn; **24:** Mansa Musa I–McBride, Angus (1931-2007) / Private Collection / © Look and Learn / Bridgeman Images; pattern–Apolinarias/Shutterstock.com; **25:** Mali background–Michele Alfieri; Mecca–Zurijet) Shutterstock.com; **26:** Mosque of Djenné–trevor kittelty/Shutterstock.com; **27:** Catalan Atlas–Catalan Atlas; Timbuktu–Antonio Abrignani/Shutterstock.com; **28:** [swirl–Apolinarias; dots–Tatiana Kasyanova; leaves–vectorOK; zigzag–nikifiva; lines–Mikhaylova Liubov; diamond–Annykos; triangle–Alextanya; scribble–Taani; orange–Alextanya; sewn–Mikadun; grid–De-V; brown–Vasilius; circle–vectorOK] Shutterstock.com; **31:** [road–Andrzej Kubik; lady–Kirsz Marcin] Shutterstock.com; **32:** [bricks–2630ben; background–Kues; frame–rangizzz; goats–Andrzej Kubik; ruins–2630ben] Shutterstock.com; Great Zimbabwe–Tips Images/Superstock; **33:** [boy–Samuel Borges Photography; monkeys–JPL Designs] Shutterstock.com; wall–Robert Harding Picture Library/ Superstock; **34:** [doorway–2630ben; boy with backpack–Samuel Borges Photography; boy with yellow shirt–SergiyN] Shutterstock.com; **35:** [bricks border–2630ben; soapstone bird–agap] Shutterstock.com; **36:** [background–marina_ua; bone texture–PinkPueblo] Shutterstock.com; Lebombo mountains–Megan Little; **37:** Ishango bone–Ben2; Rhind Mathematical Papyrus–Paul James Cowie; Timbuktu Mathematical Manuscripts / EuroAstro; **38:** [hieroglyphs–Bernice Williams; rocks–Daniel Smolcic] Shutterstock.com; **40:** calligraphy–Hosatte Jean-Marie/ ABACA/Newscom; pattern–EV-DA/Shutterstock.com; Boubacar Sadeck–Mamadou/ everythingspossible.wordpress.com; [spots–donatas1205; old paper–fotorro] Shutterstock.com; **41:** manuscripts–Mamadou/everythingspossible.wordpress.com; **42:** burnt manuscripts–ERIC FEFERBERG/AFP/Getty Images; **44:** [ruins–kravka; paper–Robyn Mackenzie; twine–Picsfive] Shutterstock.com; Marishana Mabusela–courtesy of Marishana Mabusela; **45:** Al Khazneh–Bernard Gagnon; trowel–detchana wangkheeree/Shutterstock.com; **46:** excavation site–courtesy of Marishana Mabusela; **47:** surveying find–courtesy of Marishana Mabusela; [tape measure–Seregam; shovel–Ozaiachin] Shutterstock.com.